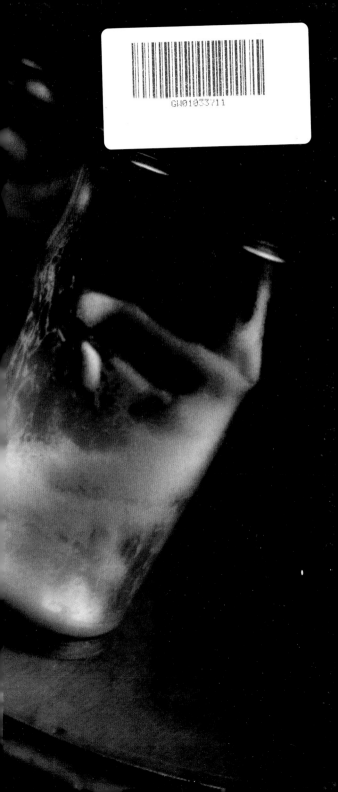

Editor: Sonya Sparks

Design: Cobalt Design

Illustrations: Brian Fitzgerald

Photography Frontispiece: Mike O'Toole

Maps: by kind permission of the Ordnance Survey of Ireland.

Printed by Elkar Artes Graficas S. Coop., Larrondo Beheko Etorbidea 4, 48180 Loiu, Spain.

The publishers wish to thank the Proprietors, Bar Managers and Staff of each pub for their assistance.

Many thanks to Dublin Tourism for their assistance.

www.visitdublin.com

Dublin Tourism Offices:
Dublin Tourism Centre, Suffolk Street, Dublin 2.
O'Connell Street, Dublin 1.
Baggot Street Bridge, Dublin 2.
Arrivals Hall, Dublin Airport.
Dun Laoghaire Ferry Terminal.
The Square, Tallaght, Dublin 24.

Published by Hotel Solutions Ltd.,
13 Windsor Place, Dublin 2. Ireland.
Tel: 662 3700 Fax: 662 3722

ISBN: 0-9540809-5-5

THE OFFICIAL
DUBLIN PUB GUIDE 2003

Published by Hotel Solutions
in association with Dublin Tourism

contents

n i g h t c l u b s

"Good puzzle," James Joyce had his humble hero Leopold Bloom wonder in his remarkable novel, Ulysses, "would be cross Dublin without passing a pub." It would be practically impossible, of course. There are literally hundreds of them, peppered all around the centre, and they have played a remarkable role over the years in shaping the city's political, social, intellectual and artistic life. Revolutions, protests, great novels, plays and poems have been planned and plotted in some of the more famous of them, and the pub has always acted as a bastion of social equality and free speech in a city that was long occupied, and for a long time sternly conservative.

Dublin is probably the world's most famous drinking city, and that of course is all down to the unique atmosphere of its pubs. Although some (The Brazen Head, for instance, which may date back to the 12th century) are older, most of the city's more famous public houses date from the early or mid-19th century, and their beautiful interiors are typically high-ceilinged and ornate, with long wooden bars and huge mirrors along the walls. Their appearance, though, however admirable, is a little bit beside the point – Dublin's pubs aren't renowned for their polished brass and Victorian splendour, but for their unrivalled conviviality, wit and warmth. And, however historic or grand it may be, a pub is ultimately created by its customers, and its staff.

Unlike bars in England and elsewhere, Dublin's pubs were always privately owned, rather than the pawns of some huge brewery. This, and the fact that they were generally family-run, added to their individuality. Until the middle of the last century, most of them were male only, and predominantly working class. The city centre pubs tended to be favoured by one or other of the various trades and professions. There were actors' pubs, busdrivers' pubs, politicians' pubs and dockers' pubs. There were singing pubs, talking pubs and quiet, contemplative pubs. Probably the most famous of them all, though, were those favoured by the city's journalists.

Journalists tended to be extravagant drinkers, and thus the publican's best friend. The Palace Bar, on Fleet Street, was for a long time associated with The Irish Times, and during the 1940s and 50s, its star writers would gather in the wonderfully snug back room. Hacks, though, are fickle creatures, and they often defected to O'Neill's, on Suffolk Street. O'Neills had one of the most sought-after snugs in the city (snugs are walled-off little alcoves in which you

9

can sit and drink privately and gossip and plot) and, although it was extensively refurbished and extended in the early 1990s, the original front bar is just as it was.

Some of Dublin's favourite old pubs had untimely appointments with the wrecking ball during the 1970s in particular, or else were simply refurbished to death, but a good handful of the very finest remain, steadfast in a changing town. There's been a pub on the site of Mulligan's, of Poolbeg Street, since 1782, and the present building dates from the 1850s. It was a firm favourite of the now defunct Irish Press and Evening Press newspapers, as well as actors from the old Theatre Royal. The plain wooden interior has hardly changed at all since the 1920s, and has seen some eventful evenings. Mulligan's was regularly raided by the Black and Tans during the Civil War, as it was reputed to be a popular haunt for IRA men. John F. Kennedy drank in here as a young man, as did Bing Crosby and Gracie

Fields. A crowd calling themselves the 'Society for the Preservation of the Dublin Accent' also met regularly here, and no better place for them.

Mulligan's, though, is most famous for its unfailingly excellent pint, and when I first started drinking there in the early 1980s, it was still highly unusual to see anyone (including the women) drinking anything other than Guinness. On busy nights half of the bar counter would be taken up by regimental lines of three-quarters full, settling pints, and no one said 'Can I have two pints of...', they just said 'Two pints.' All the Irish Press newspapers are gone now, but some of the seasoned veterans of those organs still drift in from time to time, and a framed picture on the wall commemorates the patronage of perhaps the most famous of them, legendary sports writer, Con Counihan.

Another hallowed Dublin institution is the

Dublin Tourism

Step into a World of History & Culture - VISIT...

DUBL!N™

1. **Malahide Castle** Malahide, Co. Dublin
   Tel: + 353 1 846 2184 Fax: + 353 1 846 2537

2. **Dublin Writers Museum** 18 Parnell Square, Dublin 1
   Tel: + 353 1 872 2077 Fax: + 353 1 872 2231

3. **James Joyce Museum** Sandycove, Co. Dublin
   Tel: + 353 1 280 9265 Fax: + 353 1 280 9265

4. **The Shaw Birthplace** 33 Synge Street, Dublin 8
   Tel: + 353 1 475 0854 Fax: + 353 1 872 2231

5. **Fry Model Railway** Malahide Castle, Demense, Co. Dublin
   Tel: + 353 1 846 3779 Fax: + 353 1 846 3723

www.visitdublin.com

aforementioned Palace Bar, with its beautiful old wooden
interior and its uniquely intimate panelled parlour. On
weekend nights the Palace teems with tourists and party
animals on their way into or out of Temple Bar, but not so
long ago it was sleepy enough to have its own resident cat,
who would appear in the back room on sunny mornings
and lick the cream off the head of your pint, if you let him.
And more on the Palace in a moment.

The Old Stand, on Exchequer Street, lays claim to one of
the most distinguished lineages of any drinking house in the
town. It gets its name from the Old Stand at Lansdowne
Road, and has always been popular with sports enthusiasts,
but its history stretches back considerably further than
that. There's been a pub here since at least 1659, when
Charles II, no less, renewed the licence, but evidence
suggests that a licence existed for an
establishment on exactly the
same site at

least 200 years previous to that. You'll be pleased to hear that the interior has been altered somewhat since the 15th century, but its wooden interior and fine Welsh dressers make it a very comfortable place to stop off in for a pint.

A richly traditional Dublin pub experience in the suburbs can be found at Taylor's Three Rock Bar, on the Grange Road in Rathfarnham. This charming, no-nonsense pub runs an Irish Night every night of the week, complete with a rousing resident band, the Merry Ploughboys, who provide an evening of song, ballads, music and dancing in a uniquely convivial atmosphere. There's food, too, if the whole thing gets too much for you.

We've been talking here of course about the traditional Dublin pub, beloved institutions that have been run in more or less the same way for generations. But, over the past five or six years, Dublin has suddenly changed almost beyond recognition. A fairly sleepy city has become a humming hive of industry, and the pub scene has been affected as profoundly as every other aspect of Dublin life. The old bars are still there, of course, but alongside them now are a bewildering array of sumptuous and imaginatively decorated lounges, clubs and cafés. Purists may moan, but I think this is a very positive development. Dublin now has a genuine choice as to where and how it will drink, and the presence of these new, dimly-lit cosmopolitan hangouts only makes you appreciate the older institutions when you go back to them.

And besides, the essence of the Dublin pub has nothing to do with wooden bars and brass fittings. It's more about mood than décor. There's a sort of unwritten law in Dublin that pubs must be tolerant and convivial places, in which differences are put aside along with the cares of everyday life, and a brief moment of garrulous fun can be had. Laughter is the commonest noise you'll hear in any pub around this city, which is a sure sign that these are the places in which Dubliners truly relax. The true Dublin pub is a mood, not a building, and that mood can exist in the newest as easily as in the oldest of our city's bars.

For some strange reason, Irish writing and alcohol have always been fairly inextricably linked, and Dublin's pubs have played a huge role in the fortunes of its many celebrated writers. While other European cities had cafés and restaurants in which their artists, writers and critics could meet, Dublin only ever had its pubs. In a generally poor city, there was no restaurant culture to speak of, and the idea of sitting outside and sipping coffee must have seemed ludicrous, so that only left the long bars and dark corners of the pubs for those who wanted to think and talk. And as Dublin has produced a phenomenal number of notable writers over the years, a lot of its pubs have proud literary associations.

Perhaps Dublin's most famous literary pub scene took place in a pub that no longer exists. Barney Kiernan's used to be in Stoneybatter, behind the Four Courts, and it was there that Joyce set the 'Cyclops' episode of his great novel,

Ulysses. It tells of a the disastrous meeting between Leopold Bloom and a hypocritical old patriot called the Citizen, which ends in a fight, flight and the throwing of a biscuit tin. Joyce used another pub as a key setting in his epic novel – Davy Byrne's, of Duke Street, which happily is still very much alive. It was there that "the wandering Jew," as Joyce called Bloom, stopped off on that long June day for his lunch. He had a gorgonzola sandwich, and a glass of Burgundy, and every June 16th gangs of people in period dress pile into the pub to eat and drink the same meal, as part of the Bloomsday celebrations.

As Joyce's own drinking life in Dublin was quite short (he left for Europe in 1904, aged 22, and hardly returned), he was sometimes dependent on the stories of others for his information. The stories of his father, John, must have been of great help to him, for Joyce senior must have drank in most of the Dublin pubs that existed at the end of the 19th century. He loved Parnell, singing, arguing and drinking, and frittering away his  family's meagre fortune indulging those passions. There are stories of him indulging his many passions in various hostelries both extant and long forgotten all over central Dublin around the turn of the century, but these acccounts are hard to verify.

A more reliable Joycean connection can be claimed by The Duke, on Duke Street, in that there is incontestable evidence that the great writer himself actually took a drink here. It was here, 1912 (though the pub at that time was called Kennedy's), that Joyce met James Stephens, author of The Crock of Gold, and memorably insulted him. Joyce told the lesser-known novelist that he should 'give up writing and take a good job like shoe-shining as a more promising profession.' Stephens responded in kind and the two parted fuming, but they later became great friends, and an old Joyce elected Stephens the only person capable of finishing Finnegans Wake in the event of his death (an honour indeed,

Bars plc

Rathmines Capital Hotel
Rathmines

Grafton Capital Hotel
Lower Stephens St

Trinity Capital Hotel
Pearse St

Bobs
East Essex St

Break for the Border
Lower Stephens St

Café en Seine
Dawson St

Fireworks
Tara St

Down Under in Major Toms
South King St

O'Dwyers
Lower Mount St

Planet Hollywood
St Stephen's Green

Savannah
Rathmines

Sinnotts
South King St

Sosueme
South Great Georges St

Coyote Lounge
D'Olier St

The George
South Great Georges St

Zanzibar
Ormond Quay

Capital Bars Pub Trail

Zanzibar

River Liffey

Bobs

Fireworks

Coyote
Lounge

Trinity Capital Hotel

The George

Sosueme

Break for the
Border

Café en Seine

Grafton Capital Hotel

Down Under
(in Major Toms)

O'Dwyers

Sinnotts

Planet Hollywood

Grand Canal

Savannah

Rathmines Capital Hotel

www.capitalbars.com

though Stephens must have been terrified at the prospect of ever actually being called on to attempt that task).

Toner's, on Lower Baggot Street, is the place where Oliver St John Gogarty brought the decidedly upper class W.B. Yeats, who had decided he wished to visit a pub. It's difficult to imagine the lanky and bespectacled poet feeling at his ease in such salty surroundings. According to Gogarty, the great man stood at the bar and drank a sherry in silence, surrounded by the noise and chatter of that lively bar, then turned to his friend and said, 'I have seen a pub. Will you kindly take me home.' There is no record of the Senator ever taking a notion to visit one again.

The crowd at the always busy McDaid's of Harry Street these days is a heady mix of students and younger tourists, but it was once the most celebrated literary pub in the city. In the 1950s, it was the epicentre of Dublin's Bohemian literary scene, and its list of celebrated regulars included Patrick Kavanagh, Brendan Behan, J.P. Donleavy, Anthony Cronin and John Ryan. Ryan pulled together his influential literary magazine, Envoy, along the bar, Behan started fights and stood on tables to sing, while Kavanagh quietly lectured everyone on the virtues of the Greeks. Flann O'Brien dropped in from time to time too, but always departed before things got too rowdy - he did not like the noise of night time.

It was in McDaid's that the first ever Bloomsday celebration was planned. Organised by John Ryan, the participants included O'Brien, Kavanagh and the young poet, Anthony Cronin. They set off early on the morning of June

16th, 1954, aiming to follow the steps across Dublin of Stephen Daedalus and Leopold Bloom, but they only got as far as Sandymount Strand before the group

parted in disarray. Plenty of drink had been taken, which had probably helped the natural emnity between Kavanagh and O'Brien to emerge. The trend caught on, though, and the Bloomsday circus gets bigger every year.

Kavanagh tended to favour the pubs along Baggot Street. The legendarily eccentric and sometimes difficult Monaghan poet lived nearby, and would often drop in to one or other of them during the day on his way to and from the betting shops, gazing myopically at the newspaper through his fish bowl spectacles and glaring at anyone who had the effrontery to directly address him.

Flann O'Brien drank practically everywhere over the years, usually because he had to. He too was, well, unpredictable when drinking, and often ended up being

barred for his spirited vocal character assassinations of those around him. There was a story about him meeting a friend of his from the sports desk of the Irish Times on Westmoreland Street, and asking him to go for a drink. When the friend agreed, O'Brien apparently said, "Well we'll have to go to Swords, then – I'm barred from everywhere else." O'Brien celebrated pubs and drinking throughout his work, both as a remarkable columnist in the Irish Times, and as the author of a number of wonderfully surreal comic novels; but drink also took over his life, and he died at 54.

As a young writer, Flann O'Brien's favourite haunt was The Palace, on Fleet Street. It was here, in the 40s and early 50s, that the legendary Irish Times editor, R.M. Smyllie, held court and distributed the following day's newspaper assignments. Austin Clarke, Brinsley McNamara, Patrick Campbell and T.H. White were among his acolytes, and the plain but comfortable back room became a kind of intellectual court, and a pretty bawdy one at that. John Ryan recalled in his book, Remembering How We Stood, that "heavier or more sustained drinking than took place in the Pearl [a neighbouring pub, now long gone] or the Palace during those years may never have occurred before or will again – it is still remembered with awe by old-timers. It might have had something to do with the war, for there was little to spend money on and, as I have said, drink itself was not scarce. Chat never is in Dublin, and we can only imagine what novels and poems and plays drifted up and lodged with the nicotine In the ceilings of those hostelries."

That's well said, and could be said of any of Dublin's great literary pubs, where talk was always cheap, and a lot easier than actually writing.

Visitors to modern Dublin who come expecting a cosy, homogenous world of wooden bars with big mirrors, sawdust floors and long counters against which dozens of flat-capped old men are leaning, nurturing half empty pints of Guinness, are in for something of a surprise. And I for one think it's a very pleasant surprise. Over the past five years, in case you didn't know, the city has experienced an unprecedented period of growth, and that boom has been reflected in the creation of a whole new generation of Dublin bars designed to meet the needs of a new, affluent and increasingly cosmopolitan wave of Dubliners.

When I was young and starting to drink, back in the early 1980s, there were only the celebrated, old-fashioned bars of yore to choose from. They were magnificent, with their characters and faded décor and time-honoured ways, but as a late teen and early twenty-something, it would have been nice to have been given a choice. If the young me had been mysteriously transported by time machine to the year 2001, I would have thought I'd died and gone to heaven. The variety of styles, sizes and types of new pub is genuinely and wonderfully bewildering, and makes you think more of New York or Tokyo or Berlin than the comfortable, predictable old Dublin you grew up with.

I had lived away from Ireland and only returned midway through our remarkable boom, and the first sign I saw that things were definitely changing was when I visited

two newish hotels on either side of the river. The Clarence, on the south quays, had been famously bought by U2 in the mid-1990s and given a complete facelift. That facelift included the now well-established Octagon Bar, with its wonderful wooden bar floating in the centre of an open room. Some dislike the absence of windows in the main bar, but I for one fell in love with it on sight. The lighting is sombre and bluish, the music, as you'd expect, subtle and impeccably chosen, and the atmosphere is remarkably relaxed and unhurried. It gets really busy now, on weekend nights, but on Sundays, or during the week, it's one of the best places to meet for a chat. And yes, the owners do sometimes drink there.

The departure from the Dublin norm was if anything even more spectacular in the starkly elegant Morrison Hotel, just across the river. The lighting is even subtler in here (we all look better in that), and the décor is a compelling mix of eastern and Scandinavian influences. There are two bars as you enter the hotel, a brighter, more open one on your right, and a more mysterious, nook-filled one on your left. Pole position in this bar is on one of the huge black and white

leather chairs that are tastefully arranged near a window looking onto the busy quay. And somehow it makes you feel all the more relaxed watching the rest of the world hurrying about its business – you feel as though you're getting away with something. It seems almost silly drinking stout in here – oddly-coloured cocktails and bottles of chilled wine are much more the norm.

The Viperoom, back across the Liffey near O'Connell Bridge, is more than just a great name. Downstairs is a hopping club that we are too old to enter, but upstairs is a long, thin, elegant bar that makes you think of New York City. On some nights, live jazz emanates from a cramped stage at the back, and you really have to pinch yourself to remind yourself of where you are. Speaking of New York, Huey from the Fun Lovin' Criminals first came to Dublin a few years back and seems to have fallen in love with the place. He has opened an equally funky bar called Voodoo, down the river beyond Capel Street, which he sometimes frequents himself.

Perhaps the nicest thing about some of these new bars is the strange places they spring up in. Take Fireworks, for example, a remarkably imaginative and attractive-looking new bar in the shell of what used to be Dublin's Central Fire Station. This beautifully designed three-storybar and club with a capacity of 1200 has transformed a previously quiet part of Tara Street. Zanzibar, opened a few years back, played a vital part in the rejuvenation of Ormond Quay, on the north quays. That area is now among the very busiest on weekend nights, and Zanzibar is the star attraction, a plush, dimly lit bar with a sumptuous, eastern interior and a really unusual atmosphere.

Without exaggeration, Café en Seine must be one of the most staggeringly beautiful bars in all of Europe. Just recently refurbished, this cavernous bar is decorated in a wonderfully opulent 19th century French style, with glass-panelled ceilings, a French hotel lift, 40 ft trees, a Louis XIV bust and a marvelous wood and marble bar lined with huge glass lamps. It's a joy to drink in, and enough to make you lose the run of yourself altogether and decide that, if you're drinking in here, you must be a very important person altogether. By sharp contrast, Sosume, one of Dublin's newest bars, is all stylish mimimalism, with lots of bamboo, Buddhist statues, Japanese paintings and a v. stylish crowd. That said, the atmosphere is nice and relaxed, and the bar boasts a selection of more than 50 beers from around the world.

In Cocoon, back up in town near the Hibernian Mall, everyone looks cool and dresses in leather and blends in ominously with the upholstery, telling you that this is a very hip spot to be seen in indeed. The old Harp Bar, on a corner on the southside of O'Connell Bridge, used to

Café En Seine

39/40 Dawson Street, Dublin 2

Pub of the Year

- Winner of the Georgina Campbell/Jameson Pub of the Year 2003
- Open daily from 10.30a.m. serving coffee & pastries
- Full lunch & evening menu
- Jazz brunch every Sunday afternoon
- Live Jazz/Swing every Monday night
- Extensive wine and Cocktail lists

39/40 Dawson Street, Dublin 2
Tel: 01 6774567   Fax: 01 6774488
Email: cafeenseine@capitalbars.com
Web Address: www.capitalbars.com

enjoy a very dubious reputation indeed. It closed a few years back, and the space has since been transformed into Q, a remarkable labyrinth of a pub on several levels with a multitude of screens, huge and small, showing music videos and so on. The noise level is extraordinary, but the place is well-designed and incredibly popular.

Night clubs in Dublin used to be synonymous with bad, overpriced wine, hilariously conservative music and lunges in the dark at half three in the morning, but those days are long gone, thanks be to God. The Sugar Club, off Stephen's Green, is a good example of a particularly imaginative modern club. It used to be an art cinema, and the owners have retained the cosy, auditorium feel. They simply removed every second row of seating in order to accommodate tables, and now you can be served by waiters as you watch a jazz band noodle away on stage. The Gaiety has long been a vital part of Dublin life, but after hours the theatre now doubles as a wonderful, multi-floored music club. There are bars on various levels, an old film showing on the stage, and you can simply wander from bar to bar as your mood takes you.

So, has this wave of brave new pubs threatened the existence of the traditional Dublin bar? I don't think so, for they seem to be able to coexist quite happily beside each other. In a way, in fact, a visit to one will only increase your appreciation for the other. Mulligan's or the Viper Room? It all depends on your mood, but a real choice is a wonderful thing.

pubs

'When no food is in your larder,
And no rashers grease your pan,
When life is black as the hour of
night, A pint of plain is your
only man…'

Flann O'Brien

Abbey Tavern

Abbey Street, Howth, Co. Dublin
Tel: 839 0307/ 839 0282/832 2006
E-mail: info@abbeytavern.ie
Web Address: www.abbeytavern.ie

CELEBRATING 40 YEARS
OF TRADITIONAL IRISH
ENTERTAINMENT

As you enter this **16th Century Tavern** you will be struck by its old world charm, authenticity and simplicity (no gimmicks) just blazing turf fires, original stone walls, flagged floors, gas lighting…a truly warm Irish welcome.

The Abbot Restaurant upstairs is renowned for its seafood, receiving supplies daily from the local harbour. Great food in unique surroundings.

The Barn offers for your entertainment the world famous Abbey Tavern singers and musicians in the traditional Irish atmosphere. This pleasant relaxed evening includes a typical four course Irish Dinner and entertainment reflecting Ireland's wealth of music and song.

"THE ORIGINAL TRADITIONAL IRISH EVENING IN DUBLIN"

Bar Food served: lunchtime, evening, vegetarian option, Sunday lunch
Credit Cards: V, MC, AE, D, L
Capacity: Restaurant 80, The Barn 200, The Bar 200

TRADITIONAL IRISH ENTERTAINMENT	m	t	w	t	f	s	s
	●	●	●	●	●	●	●

OPENING HOURS:
7 days 10.30am-12.30pm • Restaurant 7.00pm until late Mon-Sat

All Sports Café

10 Fleet Street, Temple Bar, Dublin 2
Tel: 679 3942   Fax: 679 3946
Email: allsports@themorgan.com

All Sports Café is located in Temple Bar and is one of Dublin's leading entertainment venues. The design is based on high energy, modern sports theme which includes a restaurant and fully licensed bar. We offer a wide variety of menus to suit all your catering needs. Live DJ's Thursday to Sunday to enhance your night.

Suitable for all group sizes, catering to those who seek casual dining and a vibrant party atmosphere or for the larger groups that just want to have fun.

All Sports features all major sporting events including NFL, Football and Rugby.

Food served; all day, vegetarian option
Credit Cards: V. MC. AE. D. L
Capacity: 100

LIVE DJ'S

m	t	w	t	f	s	s
			•	•	•	•

OPENING HOURS:
7 days

The Bankers

16 Trinity Street, Dublin 2
Tel: 01 6793697 Fax: 01 6714582

The Bankers is situated in the heart of Dublin, just a stones throw away from the Dublin Tourism Office. Located between Grafton Street and the ever popular Temple Bar, The Bankers offers all the advantages of a traditional Irish Pub right in the centre of the city.

Once one of Dublin's smallest pubs, The Bankers has undergone extensive changes over the years to meet the ever growing demand for traditional pubs. Come in and enjoy a full lunch or freshly made soup and sandwich or simply have a great pint in an atmosphere of undeniable charm. A quiet haven during the day but bustling every night - The Bankers has something for everyone!

At The Bankers you may call as a stranger but you will leave as a friend.

Food served: all day, vegetarian option, Sunday lunch
Credit Cards: L

OPENING HOURS:
Mon-Wed 10.00am-11.30pm • Thurs-Sat 10.30am-12.30am
Sun 12.00pm-11.00pm

Bobs Bar

35 East Essex Street, Dublin 2
Tel: 677 0945 Fax: 677 9492
E-mail: bobs@capitalbars.com
Web Address: www.capitalbars.com

Located in the heart of Temple Bar, Dublin's left bank and cultural quarter, Bobs is a contemporary stylish Irish bar.

It offers an alternative to the more traditional bars in the area covering four floors, one of which is a designated dance floor-you can enjoy a mix of great sounds till late. Great Irish hospitality and plenty of fun 7 nights til late. Try the bar food every evening til 9pm. Live music every Sunday evening from 9pm. The top floor is available for private functions.

Part of the Capital Bars group of hotels & bars.

Bar Food served: evening, vegetarian option
Credit Cards: V. MC. AE. D. L
Capacity: 1000

	m	t	w	t	f	s	s
LIVE DJ MIX OF CONTEMPORARY SOUNDS			●	●	●	●	●

OPENING HOURS:
Wed-Fri 4.00pm-2.30am • Sat-Sun 12.00pm-2.30am
Nightclub open Wed-Sun

Break For The Border

Lower Stephens Street, Dublin 2
Tel: 478 0300 Fax: 478 2910
E-mail: breakfortheborder@capitalbars.com
Web Address: www.capitalbars.com

Break For The Border, one of the best all round entertainment spots in Dublin incorporates three floors of happening "fun".

The venue features a full restaurant specialising in steaks and fajitas and also includes one whole floor with a DJ. Early bird menu Sun-Thurs 6pm-8pm. Downstairs enjoy a live music gig which transforms into a club after midnight.

Accommodation attached at the Grafton Capital Hotel.
Part of the Capital Bars group of hotels & bars.

Bar Food served: evening, vegetarian option
Credit Cards: V. MC. AE. D. I.
Capacity: 1200
Children friendly 6.00pm-8.30pm in restaurant

Live Bands & DJs, Rock, Pop & Chart	m	t	w	t	f	s	s
			•	•	•	•	

OPENING HOURS:
Sun-Tues 5.00pm-11.30pm • Wed-Fri 5.00pm-2.30am
Open all day Sat from 12.00pm-2.30am • Restaurant Mon-Sun 6.00pm-late

The Bridge Bar

Westmoreland Street, Dublin 2
Tel: 01 6355451
E-Mail: manager@bridge.bewleys.ie

Centrally located on one of Dublin's busiest streets, the Bridge
Bar offers a haven from the hustle and bustle of Westmoreland
Street. Situated at the gateway to Temple Bar, the Bridge Bar is a
spacious, lively and friendly pub with a cosmopolitan clientele.
All major sporting events are covered on the large screen, making
the Bridge a popular destination for Dubliners meeting for drinks
after work.

   After dark the Bridge Bar becomes a happening/exciting
nightspot with a large dance floor and the best sounds around.
The Bridge Bar is the perfect place for meeting old friends and
finding new ones.

Food served: lunchtime, evening
Credit Cards: V. MC. L

Live Bands & DJ's	m	t	w	t	f	s	s
		●		●	●	●	●

OPENING HOURS:
Sun-Wed 10.30am-11.30pm • Thurs 10.30am-12.30am
Fri-Sat 10.30am-2.30am

Brown's Barn

CityWest Bridge, Naas Road, Dublin 22
Tel: 464 0930 Fax: 464 0929
Email: info@brownsbarn.ie
Web Address: www.brownsbarn.ie

Modern and stylish, Brown's Barn is a new bar and restaurant situated at the CityWest Bridge on the N7 only 15 minutes from Dublin's city centre. Whether you're having a quick breakfast, enjoying a leisurely lunch or relaxing over an evening drink, the Bar & Carvery provides a welcoming ambience, conducive to enjoyable dining and good conversation.

Although steeped in history, we still found a space for a thoroughly modern Cocktail Bar, where you can order from our imaginative cocktail menu, catering for the more exotic taste-buds or just relax after your meal in our fine dining restaurant on the first floor.

The courtyard of Brown's Barn has been designed to include a trellised Beer-Garden with pine tables and benches, where you can enjoy a drink before dining (weather permitting!).

Bar Food served: all day, vegetarian option, Sunday lunch, Carvery
Credit Cards: V. MC. AE. D. L
Capacity: 600

OPENING HOURS:
Mon-Wed 10.30am-12.30am • Thurs-Sat 12.30pm-1.30am
Sunday 12.30pm- midnight

Buck Mulligans

The Burlington Hotel, Upper Leeson Street, Dublin 4
Tel: 660 5222 Fax: 668 8086

Whether enjoying a leisurely visit to Dublin or entertaining a
corporate client, look no further than Buck Mulligans bar for a
great night out. Located in the Burlington Hotel, Buck Mulligans
is a mere ten minute stroll to the heart of the city. Not that you'll
want to venture out - this multiple award-winning pub
encapsulates Dublin's unique charm and is a magnet for both locals
and visitors alike.

With an excellent carvery, which opens daily for lunch and
dinner, Buck's clever open-plan design makes it a perfect choice
for large or small gatherings. In addition to the main bar, the
"loft" area can be reserved for private functions. And, if you're in
the mood for continuing the party, walk out the door into Club
Anabel, Dublin's trendiest nightclub.

Bar Food served: lunchtime, evening, carvery
Credit Cards: V. MC. AE. D. L
Capacity: 1000

OPENING HOURS:
Sun-Thurs 11.00am-11.30pm • Fri-Sat 11.00am-12.30am
Food served 12.30pm-2.15pm & 5.30pm-8.15pm
Nightclub open Wed-Sat

Buskers

Fleet Street, Temple Bar, Dublin 2
Tel: 677 3333 fax: 677 3088
Email: buskers@tbh.ie

Enjoy the unique atmosphere of Buskers', located in the trendy and cosmopolitan Temple Bar quarter. The bright and airy bar, combines vibrant colours and soothing tones creating a relaxing and yet exciting continental style bar to suit every mood. Relax and enjoy lunch or dinner from our bar and restaurant menu available daily which includes a great brunch at the weekends.

Join in the amazing party atmosphere with our DJ's playing the coolest sounds, open late Thursday to Saturday, and on Thursday night, its free in from Buskers to **Boomerang** nightclub. Buskers is a contemporary landmark among the many famous bars and pubs of Dublin.

Bar Food served: all day, vegetarian option
Credit Cards: V. MC. AE. L.
Capacity: 750

LIVE DJ	m	t	w	t	f	s	s
8pm until close	•	•	•	•	•	•	•

OPENING HOURS:
From 11.30am 7 days
Late opening Thurs-Sat until 12.30am • Restaurant 12.30pm-9.30pm 7 days
Boomerang Nightclub open Wed-Sat night

Café En Seine

39/40 Dawson Street, Dublin 2
Tel: 01 6774567 Fax: 01 6774488
Email: cafeenseine@capitalbars.com
Web Address: www.capitalbars.com

Café En Seine is one of the most spectacular bars in Europe. This unique bar is designed in an art deco theme that incorporates features such as a Louis XIVth bust, a French hotel lift and a glass atrium with real 40 ft trees. You feel you are back in the heady days of early 19th Century Paris.

Always buzzing and loved by the Dublin social set, with a selection of live jazz and swing bands. Open from 10.30am every day serving fresh pastries and an extensive lunch menu. Try the Sunday Brunch and enjoy live Jazz every Monday at 10pm. Winner of the Jameson/Georgina Campbell Pub of the Year.

Part of the Capital Bars group of hotels & bars.

		m	t	w	ᴸ	ᶠ	ᴈ	ᴱ
Live Jazz & Swing Bands		•						•

Food served: vegetarian option, carvery
Credit Cards: V. MC. A. D. L.

OPENING HOURS:
Mon-Wed 9.00am-12.30am • Thurs-Sat 9.00am-2.30am

Cocoon Bar & Cocktail Lounge

Royal Hibernian Way, Duke Lane, Dublin 2
Tel: 01 679 6259 Fax: 01 679 6540
E-mail: office@cocoon.ie
Web Address: www.cocoon.ie

Cocoon is a modern stylish bar with the emphasis on
comfortable luxurious surroundings. Located just 20 metres off
Grafton Street, it is an ideal location to unwind with a coffee and
mouthwatering pastries during the day.

Cocoon offers an extensive champagne range, cocktails, malt
whiskies and cigars. After dark Cocoon becomes a mecca for
visiting celebrities, top models and trendy Dubliners.

Open late Thursday to Saturday our top DJ's will keep you
entertained until the early hours.

Dress code smart casual.

Food served: lunchtime
Credit Cards: V. MC. L
Children Friendly: until 4.00pm

Live DJ	m	t	w	t	f	s	s
				●	●	●	

OPENING HOURS:
7 days from 12 noon • Late opening Thurs, Fri & Sat

Coyote Lounge

21 D'Olier Street, Dublin 2
Tel: 671 2089 Fax: 671 5759
E-mail: coyotelounge@capitalbars.com
Web Address: www.capitalbars.com

This bar and club is located on a busy thoroughfare directly in the centre of the city. Coyote Lounge offers a sophisticated and stylish bar and club with a mediterranean feel, lots of cosy alcoves and a large wine and cocktail list. A laid back spot till 11 when it kicks into a lively club featuring top DJs playing a mix of music from R 'n B to chart, dance and retro. One of the most popular clubs in Dublin which hosts a number of big name international DJs. Available for private parties and corporate events.

Part of the Capital Bars group of hotels & bars.

Credit Cards: V. MC. AE. D. L
Capacity: 1000

	m	t	w	t	f	s	s
LIVE DJ FUNKY, CHART, R&B DANCE			●	●	●	●	

OPENING HOURS:
Wed-Sat 9.00pm-3.00am • Sun 9pm until late

Davy Byrnes

21 Duke Street, Dublin 2
Tel: 677 5217 Fax: 671 7619
E-Mail: info@davybyrnespub.com
Web Address: www.davybyrnespub.com

A world famous pub, Davy Byrnes has been frequented by writers, artists, politicians and Dubliners for generations and was
immortalised by James Joyce in 'Ulysses'. Noted for its seafood
menus, traditional Irish fare and open sandwiches. Art deco in
design, the pub has paintings and sculptures by famous Irish
artists. Davy Byrnes first opened as a pub in 1798 and is
owned by the Doran family since 1942.

Bloomsday on the 14th June every year is celebrated in Davy
Byrnes with the traditional Leopold Bloom lunch of a glass of
Burgundy and a gorgonzola cheese sandwich. Readings from
'Ulysses' and customers dressed in Edwardian style create a
unique occasion on that day.

Bar Food served: all day, Sunday lunch
Credit Cards: V. MC. L
Capaacity: 150
Children over 8 years old allowed only

OPENING HOURS:
11.00am-12.30am 7 days

Doheny & Nesbitt

5 Lower Baggot Street, Dublin 2.
Tel: 676 2945 Fax: 492 5395
Email: themangangroup@eircom.net

One of Dublins oldest pubs, situated in the heart of Dublin city centre, this listed building has many unique and interesting architectural features. Doheny and Nesbitts is a haunt for many of the country's leading politicians, media personalities, artists and writers and boasts three levels of living history, the finest of food and the best of drinks.

What attractions contribute to this pub's character are debated by many; its perfect pint of stout, its array of Irish whiskeys, its comforting dark mahogany and glass furnishings, its reverence for the barman-customer relationship. What is in no doubt is that it is hot on the hit-list of tourists' and locals' itineraries - a 'must visit' whilst in Dublin.

Bar Food served: lunchtime, evening, vegetarian option
Credit Cards: V. MC. AE. D. L
Capacity: 300

OPENING HOURS:
7 days • Late night opening Fri & Sat

Down Under in Major Toms

South King Street, Dublin 2
Tel: 478 3266 Fax: 478 3423
E-mail: majortoms@capitalbars.com
Web Address: www.capitalbars.com

Dublins first Antipodean bar, located just off Grafton Street, this is definitely a "must visit" bar for everyone who likes "fun". Specialising in Australian beers - you can party till late 7 nights. You can find all things, Australian, South African and New Zealand.
Shows all major sporting events from "Down Under".
Great selection of drink promotions.

Part of the Capital Bars group of hotels & bars.

Credit Cards: V. MC. AE. D. L

LIVE DJ

m	t	w	t	f	s	s
●	●	●	●	●	●	●

OPENING HOURS:
Mon-Fri 5.00pm-2.30am • Sat 10.30am-2.30am • Sun 12.30pm-2.00am

Dublin's Left Bank Bar

Anglesea Street, Temple Bar, Dublin 2
Tel: 671 1822 Fax: 671 7637
E-mail: info@gogartys.ie
Web Address: www.gogartys.ie

Dublin's Left Bank Bar adjacent to the 'Oliver St. John Gogarty' is a trendy late night bar with a difference.

The original building was once part of the Central Bank of Ireland, the centre of the national financial district and held Ireland's gold bullion reserve in its vaults.

Witness for yourself the specially moulded coins in the ceilings and walls and the gold bars adorning the Vault Bar. Many of the original features still remain to this day.

You can relax in the comfort of these unique surroundings and enjoy a drink where Ireland's wealth was once safely hoarded.

Dublin's Left Bank Bar is open 7 nights a week with music playing from the 60s, 70s and 80s. So call in and experience it for yourself.

Bar Food served: all day, vegetarian option
Credit Cards: V. MC. D. L
Capacity: 300 bar

OPENING HOURS:
12.00pm-2.30am 7 days • Restaurant 12.00pm-12.00am

Duffy's

Main Street, Malahide, Co. Dublin
Tel: 845 0735   Fax: 845 1160

Duffy's, established in 1969, is situated in the picturesque seaside village of Malahide. It is ideally located within 10 minutes drive from Dublin Airport and only 20 minutes from Dublin city.

Duffy's interior shows an exquisite blend of South American pine and oak which is used extensively throughout. The establishment boasts an area known as "The Library"- a rare phenomena in Dublin pubs, also "The Marquee", which is a conservatory with a full wall mural of the beach in Malahide.

Bar Food served: lunchtime, Sunday lunch
Capacity: 400
Children Friendly: up to 7.00pm

TRADITIONAL IRISH MUSIC	m	t	w	t	f	s	s
				•			

OPENING HOURS:
10.30am-11.30pm Mon-Wed • 10.30am-12.30am Thurs-Sat
Sun 12.30-11.00pm

Eamonn Dorans

3A Crown Alley, Temple Bar, Dublin 2
Tel: 679 9114 Fax: 679 2692
Email: www.eamonndorans@tinet.ie
Web Address: www.eamonndorans.com

Eamonn Dorans opened in Temple Bar in 1994 and quickly
established itself as a must stop for visiting bands and musicians -
when in Dublin. Catering for the up and coming rock & pop bands
of Ireland on a nightly basis with club nights from 11pm - 3am.

The upstairs lounge features a more laid back bar and restaurant
with traditional music most nights between 7-10pm. Special guests
who have played have been U2, The Corrs, Fun Lovin' Criminals,
Shane McGowan, and The Happy Mondays. The restaurant boasts
the best pub grub in town. We're open late every evening so pop in for
a pint.

Bar Food served: all day, vegetarian option, Sunday lunch, carvery
Credit Cards: V. MC. AE.
Capacity: 700
Children Friendly: 11.00am-6.00pm

		m	t	w	t	f	s	s
LIVE MUSIC- ROCK 'N ROLL, TRADITIONAL & DANCE		•	•	•	•	•	•	•

OPENING HOURS:
7 days 11.00am-3.00am • Nightclub 8.00pm-3.00am

Fireworks

Old Central Fire Station, Tara Street, Dublin 2
Tel: 648 1099 Fax: 648 1098
E-mail: fireworks@capitalbars.com
Web Address: www.capitalbars.com

A spectacular bar/club located in a renovated fire station, this three floor venue has a capacity for 1,000 people. One of the most popular venues in Dublin where you can enjoy a game of pool, or have a snack in the early evening to the funkiest tunes. For club goers the venue is electric with top DJs after 11. You won't find anything else as hip and happening. A great mix of Club nights featuring top DJs, Saturday is a full on night of dance with DJs from 8pm, DJ Rory Lynam from Creamfields plays a mix of progressive dance from 11pm. 'Refuel after work party' every evening - Cocktails €5 until 8pm. Fireworks is the complete entertainment venue. Accommodation is attached at the Trinity Capital Hotel. Private and corporate bookings welcome.

Part of the Capital Bars group of hotels & bars.

Bar Food served. evening, vegetarian option
Credit Cards: V. MC. AE. D. L

	m	t	w	t	f	s	s
• Live DJs							
• Pool (4-11pm)	•	•	••	••	••	••	••
& Snack Menu (4-9pm)							

OPENING HOURS:
Sun-Tues 4.00pm-late, Wed-Sat 4.00pm-2.30am

Fitzsimons of Temple Bar

The Fitzsimons Hotel, East Essex Street, Temple Bar, Dublin 2
Tel: 6779315 Fax: 6779387
E-mail: info@fitzsimons-hotel.com
Web Address: www.fitzsimonshotel.com

No visit to Dublin is complete without experiencing Fitzsimons of Temple Bar, the city's most most vibrant, exciting & happening cosmopolitan bar restaurant & niteclub for the best in live music, song & dance. 3 floors of fun and entertainment at Dublin's number one venue.

Upstairs Bar Restaurant - Concerts of Traditional Irish music, song & dance (nightly and all day Sunday)
Main split level Bar - Guest DJs playing a mix of cool and funky sounds (nightly)
Niteclub - Deep down & dirty (Late 7 nights)

Food served: lunchtime, evening, Sunday lunch, carvery
Credit Cards: V. MC. • Capacity: 1000

	m	t	w	t	f	s	s
TRADITIONAL IRISH ●							
LIVE DJ ●	●●	●●	●●	●●	●	●	●●
NITE CLUB							

OPENING HOURS:
10.30am-2.30am 7 days

Forum Bar

Parliament Hotel, Lord Edward Street, Dublin 2
Tel: 670 8777 Fax: 670 8787
E-mail: parl@regencyhotels.com
Web Address: www.regencyhotels.com

The Forum is a newly built bar set in Temple Bar. This
traditionally styled bar has an exciting atmosphere offering
traditional surroundings with a contemporary feel. There is a
good mix of Irish people along with tourists.

Bar Food served: all day, vegetarian option
Credit Cards: V. MC. AE. L.
Children Friendly: up until 6.00pm

OPENING HOURS:
Mon-Wed & Sun 'til 11.30pm • Thurs-Sat until 12.00am

The George

South Great Georges Street, Dublin 2
Tel: 478 2983 Fax: 670 4427
E-mail: thegeorge@capitalbars.com
Web Address: www.capitalbars.com

Dublin's largest and best known gay venue, just off Dame
Street, the George incorporates both a bar and club and is
frequented by a gathering of stylists and models. You will find
some of the best entertainment in the City with frequent
appearances by International artists. Bingo on Sundays, is one
of the best alternative comedy events in Ireland.
Each night has something different on offer.

Part of the Capital Bars group of hotels & bars.

Credit Cards; V, MC. L
Capacity: 1000

Live DJ & Alternative Bands	m	t	w	t	f	s	s
			•	•	•	•	•

OPENING HOURS:
Mon-Tues 12.30pm-11.30pm • Nightclub open Wed-Sun until 2.30am

In

115-116 Coliemore Road, Dalkey, Co. Dublin
Tel: 01 275 0007 Fax: 01 275 0009
Email: info@indalkey.ie
Web Address: www.indalkey.ie

'IN' is a sophisticated, upmarket bar and restaurant in the heart of Dalkey.

Tastefully designed around a continental-style bar with luxurious leather sofas, mis-matched chandeliers and simple wooden tables, over two floors, 'IN' is the perfect place to enjoy a great meal and drink into the early hours against an eclectic mix of modern chilled-out music.

Eating 'IN' is as varied an experience with its ever-changing menu, although the food has a strong Mediterranean/Asian flavour, there are still some local favourites, like mussels in garlic, spring onion and chardonnay cream sauce.

Whatever your taste, you really should spend the night in.

Bar Food served: all day, vegetarian option
Credit Cards: V. MC. AE. L

OPENING HOURS:
Mon-Wed 11.00am-11.30pm • Thurs-Sat 11.00am-1.30am

Inn on the Green

The Fitzwilliam Hotel, St. Stephen's Green, Dublin 2
Tel: 478 7000 Fax: 478 7878
Email: enq@fitzwilliamhotel.com
Web Address: www.fitzwilliamhotel.com

Inn on the Green is a modern classic uniquely positioned on St. Stephen's Green, paces away from Grafton Street. Understated luxury, a fresh approach and impeccable service make the hotel bar at the Fitzwilliam Hotel the perfect venue for business and pleasure.

Widely known as one of the finest cocktail bars in the city, Inn on the Green also has a fine selection of cigars, brandy's and Irish whiskeys to tempt everyone from the novice to the seasoned connoisseur.

Serving modern cuisine from noon each day, the Inn on the Green is also the ideal pit stop on your tour of the city.

Welcome to the new Dublin - Welcome to Inn on the Green.

Bar Food served: all day, vegetarian option
Credit Cards: V. MC. AE. D. L.
Capacity: 100

OPENING HOURS:
Mon-Sun 10.30am-11.30pm
Late opening for residents only

The Isaac Butt Bar

Store Street, Dublin 1
Tel: 855 5021 Fax: 836 5390
E-mail: bar@isaacs.ie
Web Address: www.isaacs.ie

The Isaac Butt Bar must be among the most unique in Dublin
city centre. Three separate bars each with a distinctly different
style. Excellent bar food is served daily, guaranteed to tempt
even the most discerning of palates. Major sporting events are
shown on the big screen.

   The bar has developed a reputation for showcasing some of
the up and coming Irish bands and there is live music most
nights a week in the lower bar.

   The Isaac Butt has something for everyone and is
conveniently located opposite the central bus station just a 5
minute walk from O'Connell Street Bridge.

Bar Food served: all day, vegetarian option
Credit Cards: V. MC. L.
Capacity: 250

OPENING HOURS:
11.00am-12.30am
Late Bar on selected nights
Restaurant 12.00pm-8.00pm

Johnnie Fox's

Glencullen, The Dublin Mountains, Co. Dublin
Tel: 295 5647 Fax: 295 8911
E-mail: 7nights@johnniefoxs.com
Web Address: www.johnniefoxs.com

Reputed to be the highest pub in Ireland, Johnnie Fox's nestles
in the Dublin Mountains. Its famous seafood restaurant is
renowned for its menu and is well worth a visit. There is a
traditional "Hooley" held in the Parlour Room and features
Fox's Irish Dancing Troupe along with Traditional & Celtic
Music from some of Ireland's leading traditional groups.   Each
night in the bar there is free live music and the atmosphere and
craic are mighty.

Food served: all day, vegetarian option
Credit Cards: V. MC. AE. D. L
Capacity. 200 (pub) 150 (function room)

TRADITIONAL IRISH MUSIC	m	t	w	t	f	s	s
	●	●	●	●	●	●	●

OPENING HOURS:
7 days   Mon-Sat 10.30am-11.30pm   Sun 12.00-11.30pm
Restaurant Mon-Sat 12.00pm-10.00pm   Sun 1.00-10.00pm

The Long Stone

10-11 Townsend Street, Dublin 2
Tel: 671 8102
E-mail: info@thelongstone.com
Web Address: www.thelongstone.com

This family run public house derives its name from the history of the surrounding area. In 837 AD, Norsemen blazed a trail across the seas from Scandinavia and landed at the mouth of the river we now know as the Liffey. They erected a tall stone pillar in the sea, as was their custom to symbolise their possession of a new area of settlement. This long stone or "steyne" gave its name to one of the Liffey tributaries and in turn to the surrounding sandy plains. A modern day representation now stands at the front of nearby Pearse Street Garda Station.

The dominant feature of The Long Stone is a large stone fireplace taking the form of Boldar, the Viking God of Light. Elsewhere the decor is mainly Celtic with lavish mahogany carved bars, long colourful tapestries on the walls and archways of gnarled old trees. The ceiling is high with iron fittings adding to the banqueting atmosphere.

Credit Cards: V. MC. AE. L.
Capacity: 300

OPENING HOURS:
Mon-Wed 12.00pm-11.30pm • Thurs-Fri 12.00pm-12.30am
Sat 4.00pm-12.30am • Sun 4.00pm-11.00pm

McDaids

3 Harry Street, Dublin 2
Tel: 679 4395 Fax: 679 4852

Established since 1779 McDaids is situated off fashionable
Grafton Street close to Dublin city centre. One of the true
literary pubs of Dublin it was frequented in their time by many
of the greats of Irish literature, including Patrick Kavanagh and
Brendan Behan.

   Today McDaids retains much of the character and ambience
of an earlier age whilst still managing to maintain its tradition
of providing hospitality and fine beverages to the citizens of
Dublin. Popular with locals and tourists alike. Tables outside
(weather permitting).

Bar Food served: snacks provided all day
Capacity: 200
Seating outdoors in the summertime

OPENING HOURS:
Mon-Wed 10.30am-11.30pm • Thurs-Sat 10.30am-12.30am
Sun 12.30pm-11.00pm

The Morgan Bar

10 Fleet Street, Temple Bar, Dublin 2.
Tel: 679 3939 Fax: 679 3946
Email: sales@themorgan.com
Web Address: www.themorgan.com

New to the heart of cosmopolitan Temple Bar is **The Morgan Bar** at The Morgan Hotel, offering an elegant oasis of sophisticated style and relaxing comfort. Visitors to Temple Bar seeking the right venue for an after work, pre or post dinner drink will not want to miss the opportunity to chill out in the environs of Dublin's newest bar.

Pale beige and cream tones, polished wooden floors, soft brown leather seating, wide mirrors and comfortable red sofas provide the perfect environment for friends to gather and enjoy an exotic "Morgan Mai Tai" or a selection of carefully chosen wines and beers.

Food served: lunchtime
Credit Cards: V. MC. AE. D. L.

OPENING HOURS:
7 days • Late opening - Thurs, Fri & Sat

Mulligans

8 Poolbeg Street, Dublin 2
Tel: 677 5582
Web Address: www.mulligans.ie

The name 'Mulligan' has been associated with the licensed trade
since 1782 when the original family had their premises in
Thomas Street beside the old Cornmarket. The site had been a
pub since 1820 and was conveniently located close to the docks
and the Corn Exchange which generated huge business.
Mulligans is composed of an abundance of Victorian mahogany
and well used counter tops, and many divides, screens and dark
corners make it ideal for intimacy. A true City Centre pub, it is
the haunt of tourists, journalists, sportsmen and literati alike
and has managed to maintain its Old World feel, resisting the
psychedelic innovations of many rivals.

   John F. Kennedy visited in 1947 when he worked with the
Hearst Newspaper Dynasty. As you enter, gently greet this
homely shrine of ages which have long since returned to dust.

Children allowed before 6.30pm

OPENING HOURS:
Mon-Wed 10.30am-11.30pm
Thurs-Sat 10.30am-12.30am
Sun 12.30pm-11.00pm

O'Dwyers

Lower Mount Street, Dublin 2
Tel: 676 1718 Fax: 662 4863
E-mail: odwyers@capitalbars.com
Web Address: www.capitalbars.com

O' Dwyers features a traditional style pub interior and houses
three clubs in one venue; an opulent Club "Danse Macabre" is
located upstairs. "Howl at the Moon" with live bands is found
on the main floor and downstairs. Feel free to roam up and
down through the venue and sample all the fun. This is a very
popular venue with both locals and visitors. A live music bar
with a difference....

Part of the Capital Bars group of hotels & bars.

Food served: lunchtime, evening, carvery
Credit Cards: V. MC. AE. D. L
Capacity: 1000
Children Friendly: lunchtime and up to 8.30pm

Live Bands & Djs	m	t	w	t	f	s	s
			●	●	●	●	

OPENING HOURS:
Mon-Wed 11.00am-11.30pm • Thur-Fri 11.00am-2.30am • Sat 5.00pm-2.30a
Nightclub open Thurs-Sat

The Old Stand

37 Exchequer Street, Dublin 2.
Tel: 677 7220 Fax: 677 5849
Web Address: www.theoldstandpub.com

One of the oldest pubs in Dublin, the Old Stand has a great
sports following for rugby, racing, golf and football and gets its
name from The Old Stand in Lansdowne Road. The pub is
renowned for its convivial atmosphere, traditional Irish food
and great steaks. Two Welsh dressers are a feature of the pub
and add to the warm and friendly welcome from the staff.

   In 1659 Charles II renewed its public house licence. There is
evidence that a licence existed about 200 years before 1659 on
this exact position.

Bar Food served: all day, Sunday lunch
Credit Cards: V. MC. L
Children over 8 years old allowed only

OPENING HOURS:
11.00am-12.30am 7 days

Oliver Goldsmith's Lounge

Trinity Arch Hotel, 46-49 Dame Street, Dublin 2
Tel: 679 4455   Fax: 679 4511

Within sight of Trinity College and only minutes from St.
Stephen's Green, Dublin Castle and Grafton Street, this charming 19th century building nestles on the southern edge of the
renowned Temple Bar area, beside the Central Bank. Trinity
Arch is the ideal base both for the business traveller or those
just wishing to taste a slice of cosmopolitan Dublin life!

   Visit Oliver Goldsmith's Lounge, sample our delicious menu
and soak up the atmosphere of Dublin's premier bar. Whether
it's lunch, afternoon tea or a great late night out you're after -
Oliver Goldsmith's is the place to be!

Bar Food served: All day, vegetarian option, Sunday lunch, carvery
Credit Cards: V. MC. AE. D. L
Capacity: 400

Live Traditional	m	t	w	t	f	s	s
	•	•	•				•

OPENING HOURS:
Mon-Wed & Sun 10.00am-11.30pm
Thurs-Sat 10.00am-2.00am
Restaurant 5.30pm-8.30pm

The Oliver St. John Gogarty

Fleet Street, Temple Bar, Dublin 2.
Tel: 671 1822 Fax: 671 7637
Email: info@gogartys.ie
Web Address: www.gogartys.ie

The Oliver St. John Gogarty, situated in the heart of Temple Bar, is Dublin's most renowned Traditional Irish Bar and has received worldwide acclaim for its traditional Irish music, dancing and food.

The Oliver St. John Gogarty is also steeped in history. It is named after Dublin's most famous poet, pilot, politician and avid connoisseur of Guinness. Gogarty himself spent many nights exuding his customary wit in this very haunt. The bar counter is a relic as it was once the counter of the Green Room in the famous Theatre Royal. Even the food has flavours of history with restaurant dishes such as Trinity College Chicken which dates back to the 1800s and Ester Dunne Potato Cakes from 1857.

As you can imagine a visit to the Oliver St. John Gogarty is a unique experience which will be enjoyed by all and is guaranteed to provide fond memories.

Bar Food served: all day, vegetarian option, Sunday lunch, Carvery
Credit Cards: V. MC. D. L
Capacity: 200

Traditional Music	m	t	w	t	f	s	s
	•	•	•	•	•	•	•

OPENING HOURS:
Mon-Sun 10.30am-2.30am 7 days • Restaurant 12pm-12am

O'Neill's

2 Suffolk Street, Dublin 2.
Tel: 679 3656 Fax: 679 0689
E-mail: mike@oneillsbar.com
Web Address: www.oneillsbar.com

Conveniently situated in the heart of Dublin, opposite the Dublin Tourism Centre, O'Neill's is one of Dublin's most famous and historic pubs. O'Neill's has existed as a licensed premises for 300 years and is renowned for its ageless character, numerous alcoves, snugs, nooks and crannies.

O'Neill's is also known for its delicious food, particularly its great value carvery lunches. Meals are served seven days a week between 12pm and 8.00pm (12.00pm - 4.30pm on Fridays and 12.30pm - 10.00pm on Sundays). There is always a wide choice of dishes to choose from and the menu is changed daily. O'Neill's also has an excellent sandwich bar serving a wide choice of sandwiches all made to order.

Bar Food served: lunchtime, evening, vegetarian option,
Sunday lunch, Carvery
Credit Cards: V. MC. AE. L
Capacity: 800

OPENING HOURS:
7 Days
Regular pub opening hours

O'Shea's Bar & Monto Music Venue

O'Shea's Hotel, 19 Talbot Street, Dublin 1
Tel: 01 8365670 Fax: 01 8365214
E-mail: osheashotel@eircom.net
Web Address: www.osheashotel.com

O'Sheas Hotel is located in the heart of Ireland's thriving capital city, just minutes from O'Connell Street and Dublin's cultural centre - Temple Bar. At O'Shea's you will find a unique atmosphere, typical of a traditional Irish pub. O'Shea's is renowned the world over for its traditional Irish/folk music and dance, as well as being one of the cities busiest and most popular eating emporiums, boasting a choice of over 100 different dishes served all day in both the bar & restaurant.

Also incorporated in O'Sheas is MONTO music venue located in the basement of the hotel - once playing host to rising stars such as Phil Lynott & Thin Lizzy, Bob Geldof & The Boomtown Rats and also a very young U2 during the 70's. Now MONTO brings the best in rock/pop bands live to its venue for a new generation.

Food served. all day, vegetarian option, Sunday lunch
Credit Cards: V. MC. AM. D. L

Folk, Traditional Irish Rock/Pop Monto	m	t	w	t	f	s	s
	•	•	•	•	•	•	•

OPENING HOURS:
7 days • Late opening Thurs - Sat until 2am

O'Sullivan's Bar

Westmoreland Street, Dublin 2
Tel: 01 6355451
E-Mail: manager@bridge.bewleys.ie

O'Sullivan's traditional Irish Bar should be your first stop in Dublin. You can enjoy the great atmosphere and craic of O'Sullivan's located in the heart of the city, at the gateway to Temple Bar. If it is a few pints of the black stuff you're after, drop by any time of day or night there's a cosy corner waiting for you. There's lively traditional Irish music every night, so drop in and experience O'Sullivan's Bar, you'll be guaranteed an "Irish Welcome".

Food served: lunchtime, evening
Credit Cards: V, MC, I

LIVE BANDS & DJ's	m	t	w	t	f	s	s
	•	•	•	•	•	•	•

OPENING HOURS:
Sun-Wed 10.30am-11.30pm • Thurs 10.30am-12.30am
Fri-Sat 10.30am-2.30am

The Palace Bar

21 Fleet Street, Dublin 2
Tel: 01 6717388

Unspoilt and un-modernised, this small and unpretentious pub has a fame vastly out of proportion to its size. Established in 1823, thus making it one of Dublin's oldest pubs.

Step into the beautiful snug at the front in which many a historic meeting has taken place or the backroom with its high ceiling and ornate stained glass, where the literary stock used to gather. Kavanagh, Behan, Flann O'Brien and Harry Kernoff were regulars, thus the pub became internationally famous and became one of Dublin's great literary pubs. The Palace has strong sporting connections, whether it be hurling, football, rugby or horseracing. A great place to be on match days; the upstairs bar (open Wed - Sat) has a strong sporting feeling - resembled in its many photos, jerseys and drawings, including one of a truly famous sports journalist. Untainted and unspoilt by the passage of time - that's The Palace Bar.

Food served: lunchtime, evening
Credit Cards: V. L • Children Friendly: until 6.00pm

TRADITIONAL IRISH SESSION IN UPSTAIRS BAR	m	t	w	t	f	s	s
			●				●

OPENING HOURS:
Mon-Wed 10.30am-11.30pm • Thurs-Sat 10.30am-12.30am
Sun 12.30pm-11.00pm

The Porterhouse

16-18 Parliament Street, Dublin 2
Tel: 679 8847 Fax: 670 9605
E-mail: mail@porterhousebrewco.com
Web Address: www.porterhousebrewco.com

The Porterhouse is a shrine to beer, food, live music and overall, a good time. Good times and good drink are important to them and that reflects in the enjoyment people have. It is certainly helped by the fact that the Porterhouse brew some of the finest beers in the world, indeed Porterhouse Plain Porter won best stout in the world 1998/99 at the worlds 'Brewing Oscars'. Great food served both lunch and evening, followed by live music seven nights a week with afternoon sessions on Saturday and Sunday. Jameson Pub of the Year 1999. Irish Stout of the Year 2001.

Bar Food served: all day, lunchtime, evening
Credit Cards: V. MC. L
Capacity: 400
Children friendly: before 7.00pm

LIVE MUSIC-		m	t	w	t	f	s	s
TRADITIONAL ○			●		●		●	●
BLUES ●		●		●		●		
COVER BANDS ●							●●	●●

OPENING HOURS:
Mon-Wed 12.00pm-11.30pm • Thurs 12.00pm-12.30am
Fri-Sat 12.00pm-2.30am • Sun 12.30pm-11.00pm

The Queens

12 Castle Street, Dalkey, Co. Dublin
Tel: 01 2854569 Fax: 01 2858345
Email: queens@clubi.ie

Established in 1745, this makes The Queens one of Ireland's
oldest hostelries. The bar is situated in the heart of Dalkey village,
next door to the Heritage Centre. Our award-winning bar carries
on the finest tradition of providing the very best in cuisine,
convivial enjoyment and service in a unique atmosphere.

Open fires and wood features are the key welcome notes of our
bars in winter, while the sun drenched patios are an enjoyable
break in the summers days.

Bank Holiday nights are Special Party Nights with strong theme
features. Sporting events are a speciality at the Queen's Bars.

Food served: all day, vegetarian option, Sunday lunch
Credit Cards: V. MC. AE. D. L
Capacity: 200
Children friendly: up to 6pm

OPENING HOURS:
12.00-12.30pm 7 days

Savannah Café Bar & Club

Lower Rathmines Road, Dublin 6
Tel: 491 0601 Fax: 491 0609
E-mail: savannah@capitalbars.com
Web Address: www.capitalbars.com

Savannah is a very chic continental style cafe bar just a few minutes
stroll from Dublin's city centre. Relax in the intimate and stylish
bar, have lunch or dinner. Enjoy the club Thursday to Sunday
where we play a great selection of sounds till 2am. Live Jazz Band
every Wednesday night from 10pm. Bar food served 7 days from
3pm - 9pm; carvery lunch Monday to Friday 12.00 - 2.30pm and
food served all day Saturday & Sunday. Come and savour the great
atmosphere at Savannah. Accommodation attached at the
Rathmines Capital Hotel.
Part of the Capital Bars group of hotels & bars.

Food served: all day, vegetarian, bar menu, carvery
Credit Cards: V. MC. AE. D. L.
Capacity: 800 • Children Friendly: until 5.00pm

LIVE DJ FUNKY, CHART, R&B	m	t	w	t	f	s	s
				●	●	●	●

OPENING HOURS:
Nightclub open Thurs-Sun until 2.30am

Sinnotts

South King Street, Dublin 2
Tel: 478 4698 Fax: 478 2598
E-mail: sinnotts@capitalbars.com
Web Address: www.capitalbars.com

Sinnotts is a traditional style literary bar, with a large collection
of original literary pictures and prints adorning the walls. It is a
friendly and hospitable bar with music 7 nights a week.
Sinnotts is renowned for our carvery lunch, evening food and
great pints! You can also watch all the major sporting events on
our big screens. A great bar with a buzzing atmosphere!

Part of the Capital Bars group of hotels & bars.

Bar Food served: lunchtime, evening, vegetarian option, carvery
Credit Cards: V. MC. AE. D. L

Live DJ	m	t	w	t	f	s	s
	●	●	●	●	●	●	●

OPENING HOURS:
7 days until late

Smyth's of Malahide

New Street, Malahide, Co. Dublin
Tel: 8450960 Fax: 8168389
Web Address: www.smyths.ie

Hello and welcome to Smyth's of Malahide, one of Dublin's most distinctive and traditional family-run pubs! This repository of liquid culture and heritage has been dispensing hospitality to the people of Dublin for over 100 years. Idyllically located in the historic seatown of Malahide, and within 10 minutes of Dublin Airport, Smyth's is the pioneering home of Ireland's first ever All-American food concept. Using only 100% farm-reared Irish beef, Smyth's offer the best Chargrilled Steaks and Burgers in town, authentic Buffalo Wings and award-winning Baby Back Ribs and Taco Salads. Diners can enjoy the gentle sounds of Traditional Irish Music and Ballads throughout the tourist season.

Food served: all day, vegetarian option
Credit Cards: V. MC. AE. D. L • Capacity. 400

IRISH MUSIC & BALLADS	m	t	w	t	f	s	s
	●	●	●	●			

OPENING HOURS:
10.30am-11.30pm Mon-Wed
10.30am-12.30pm Thurs-Sat • 12.30pm-11pm Sunday

Sosume

South Great Georges Street, Dublin 2
Tel: 01 4781590 Fax: 01 4781156
Email: sosume@capitalbars.com
Web Address: www.capitalbars.com

Sosume is one of Dublin's newest bars, as the name suggests the bar is based on an Eastern theme with lots of bamboo and Eastern statues.

This is a stylish and modern bar popular with a trendy crowd. Sosume boasts a selection of over 50 beers from all over the world. Check out the large selection of Japanese paintings.

Live Jazz every Sunday evening from 7pm, no admission. Ask to see the extensive cocktail list, one of the best on Georges Street.

Part of the Capital Bars group of hotels & bars.

Credit Cards: V. MC. L.

Live DJ	m	t	w	t	f	s	s
				•	•	•	

OPENING HOURS:
Mon-Fri 5.00pm-2.30am • Sat 2.00pm-2.30am • Sun 4.00pm-1.00am

The Temple Bar

47/48 Temple Bar, Temple Bar, Dublin 2
Tel: 672 5287 Fax: 496 8409
E-mail: flannerys@eircom.ie

A lively, fun and exciting pub with live traditional Irish music sessions daily with two sessions at weekends, also boasting one of the largest drinking collections of whiskey in the world. The Temple Bar is the heart of Temple Bar and a must for any visitor to Dublin.

For almost 160 years, patrons have flocked to The Temple Bar. A tradition of genuinely warm welcome, backed by first-rate modern service, is the hallmark of the friendliest spot in Dublin. Whether you are alone or with a group of friends, whether you wish to dine or just want some light refreshment and good craic, you will feel thoroughly at home at The Temple Bar. Overseas and out-of-town visitors will find our staff to be a valuable mine of information on Dublin's history and haunts.

Next to the pub is The Temple Bar Trading Co. which is a merchandise store selling official Temple Bar merchandise - T-shirts, sweatshirts, baseball caps etc. Well worth a visit!

Bar Food served: lunchtime, early evening
Credit Cards: V. MC. L   Capacity: 300

LIVE IRISH MUSIC

m	t	w	t	f	s	s
•	•	•	•	•	•	•

OPENING HOURS:
11am-12.30am 7 days

T.G.I. Friday's

St. Stephen's Green West, Dublin 2
Tel: 478 1233 Fax: 478 1550
Blanchardstown Centre, Dublin 15
Tel: 822 5990 Fax: 822 5991

T.G.I. Friday's offers a great night out with superb food and
drink, great service and a fantastic party atmosphere with an
authentic American feel. The decor, the food, the experience
are all designed to let you enjoy Friday's in a way only the
Americans can do.

Primarily a cocktail bar - our bartenders are the best in the
business, highly trained and with special flair for showbiz -
they can prepare over 500 cocktails from memory. T.G.I.
Friday's is the ideal place to relax, have a cocktail and be
entertained.

Bar & Restaurant Food served: lunchtime, evening, vegetarian option
Credit Cards: V. MC. AE. L
Coctail Bar

OPENING HOURS:
12.00pm-11.30pm 7 days

The Vathouse Bar of Temple Bar

Anglesea Street, Temple Bar, Dublin 2.
Tel: 671 5622 Fax: 671 5997
Email: blooms@eircom.net
Web Address: www.blooms.ie

The Vathouse Bar of Temple Bar is located in Blooms Hotel - one of the oldest hotels in Dublin's cultural quarter. The pub gets its name from the vat house in the Guinness Brewery, St James' Gate, Dublin. During the final stage of the brewing process, Guinness is stored in large copper vats and left to mature to allow the flavour to develop. Inside the Vathouse Bar, the walls are adorned with original Guinness memorabilia. The bar offers a warm relaxed atmosphere during the day, where visitors can unwind over a drink and watch the world go by. At night, the tempo rises, with lively Irish traditional music sessions, seven nights a week.

Bar Food served: all day, vegetarian option
Credit Cards: V. MC. AE. D. L

TRADITIONAL IRISH MUSIC	m	t	w	t	f	s	s
	•	•	•	•	•	•	•

OPENING HOURS:
10.30am-2.30am 7 days

Zanzibar

35 Lower Ormond Quay, Dublin 1
Tel: 878 7212 Fax: 878 7318
E-mail: zanzibar@capitalbars.com
Web Address: www.capitalbars.com

Zanzibar is a unique bar in Dublin and a must visit for anyone who likes a sense of the dramatic. The bar has been decorated in an eastern style with plush decor and gold leaf featuring throughout giving a very opulent feel. It is a spacious and airy bar serving a selection of food in the evenings until 9pm. As Zanzibar serves late seven nights, with live DJ's, it's a very popular spot for both the trendy locals and tourists alike. Serves a great selection of wines, imported beers and cocktails. Live Jazz Band every Sunday from 5.30pm to 7.30pm. Areas available for groups and social occasions.

Part of the Capital Bars group of hotels & bars.

Bar Food served: evening
Credit Cards: V. MC. AE
Capacity: 1500

LIVE DJ

m	t	w	t	f	s	s
●	●	●	●	●	●	●

OPENING HOURS:
4.00pm-2.30am 7 nights

nightclubs

1. Boomerang Nightclub
2. Club M
3. Gaiety Theatre, The
4. Sugar Club, The
5. Temple Bar Music Centre
6. Viperoom Theatre
   Bar & Club

Boomerang Nightclub

Temple Bar, Dublin 2.
Tel: 612 9200 Fax: 607 3088
Email: boomerang@tbh.ie

Recently refurbished, Boomerang, Dublin's favourite and
hottest nightclub is located in the heart of Temple Bar, Dublin's
premier entertainment area.

Long regarded as one of Dublin's best nightclubs with a fun,
safe and happening environment. Featuring 3 bars in a modern
style and boasting an eye catching decor second to none with
state of the art sound and lights system.

Swing into Boomerang and enjoy one of the best nights of
your life!

Credit Cards: V. MC. AE

NIGHTCLUB

	m	t	w	t	f	s	s
			•	•	•	•	

OPENING HOURS:
Open Wed-Sat @ 11.30pm

Club M

Cope Street, Temple Bar, Dublin 2
Tel: 671 5622 Fax: 671 5997
E-mail: blooms@eircom.net
Web Address: www.clubm.ie

Club M nightclub is located on the doorstep of Blooms Hotel.
Club M is safe, fun and friendly and is ranked by those in the
know as one of Dublin's finest nightclubs. Drop into Club M
during your stay in Dublin and check out the inspirational laser
light system. A visit to Dublin is incomplete without a visit to
Club M where you will enjoy great music at one of Temple
Bar's best dance venues.

Capacity: 1000

OPENING HOURS:
7 nights Mon-Thurs 11.00pm-2.30am
Fri-Sat 10.00pm-2.30am
Sun 10.30pm-1.00am

The Gaiety Theatre
Plaza Café Bar · Late Night Club

South King Street, Dublin 2
Tel: 679 5622 Fax: 677 1921
E-mail: boxoffice@gaietytheatre.com
Web Address: www.gaietytheatre.com

The Plaza Café Bar is located on the plaza outside the majestic Gaiety Theatre. Seconds from the bustle of Grafton Street, under the elegance of the Victorian-style canopy and the fully refurbished Gaiety facade, this cafe-bar will offer refreshments throughout the day in the most stylish surroundings in Dublin.

The Gaiety Theatre Night Club is open on Friday and Saturday nights. The city's oldest theatre opens its doors to offer a vibrant - and extremely unique - late night, with 5 bars on 3 floors, live bands, DJs and a Cinema. Open from 11.15pm onwards, this is Dublin's latest-serving bar, with a full license until 4am both nights.

Lose yourself after midnight in Dublin's majestic Gaiety Theatre, hear some great live music, and stay out later than anywhere else.

Capacity: 750

LIVE BANDS & DJs:	m	t	w	t	f	s	s
SALSA, SOUL, FUNK, REGGAE & JAZZ					●	●	

CINEMA SHOW

OPENING HOURS:
Fri-Sat 11.15pm-4.15am

The Sugar Club

8 Leeson Street Lower, Dublin 2
Tel: 678 7188 Fax: 678 7199
E-mail: info@thesugarclub.com
Web Address: www.thesugarclub.com

"It's a venue to die for. Wood panelled walls, plush banquette seating and a pristine sound system render the rest of Dublin's night-life cruddy in comparison." *The Irish Times*, 15th Jan. 02

If you are looking for an electric atmosphere, classic cocktails and wild live music, then a visit to The Sugar Club is a must. Just on the corner of St. Stephen's Green, The Sugar Club offers a wide range of entertainment, from movies and comedy during the week to live music at the weekends. With a cocktail bar overlooking a table serviced auditorium, there's never a problem getting a drink. Catering especially to patrons over 25 years, The Sugar Club also offers private and corporate membership and bookings upon request. To go on a virtual tour visit us @www.thesugarclub.com

Credit Cards: V. MC. AE. L
Capacity: 300

	m	t	w	t	f	s	s
· Movies							
· Comedy							
• Live Music			●	●	●	●	●

OPENING HOURS:
Doors open Wed 7.30, Thurs, Fri, Sat & Sun 8.30pm
Doors close 2.00am • Serving until 3.00am every night

Taylors Irish Night

Taylors Three Rock Bar & Restaurant, Grange Road, Rathfarnham, Dublin 16
Tel: 01 4942999 Fax: 01 4946599
Email: taylorsirishnight@eircom.net
Web Address: www.taylorsthreerock.com

This is easily one of the best pub nights out in Dublin. Proprietors and musicians, the *Merry Ploughboys* ballad group, who also host this all year round two-hour show, are famous for their live performances and warm rapport with their audience. The band ensures that this is an entertaining evening of songs, ballads, music and Irish dancing with each night being different from the last depending on requests for particular songs or unexpected performances from visiting musicians. Always a great atmosphere, this no-nonsense venue represents a disappearing down-to-earth Dublin. Menus from the award-winning restaurant are available - reservations are essential - call to check show dates. 20 minutes from city centre.

Food served: lunchtime, evening, vegetarian option, Sunday lunch, Carvery
Credit Cards: V. MC. AE. D. L • Capacity: 220 at show

TRADITIONAL IRISH MUSIC & DANCING	m	t	w	t	f	s	s
	•	•	•	•	•	•	•

OPENING HOURS:
Pub: 10.30am • Taylors Irish Night: doors open 7.30pm, show time 9pm
Late bar: Friday / Saturday until 1.30am

Temple Bar Music Centre

Curved Street, Temple Bar, Dublin 2
Tel: 01 6709202 Fax: 01 6709105
Email: info@tbmc.ie Website: www.tbmc.ie

Temple Bar Music Centre, situated in the heart of Dublin city, is open 7 nights a week catering for every genre of music, dance, theatre and art, with a cafe during the day.

Since it's launch in 1996, and recently refurbished, the centre has established itself as one of the premier venues in Dublin. 'The Side Bar' is a brand new bar in a modern style, boasting wooden floors, delicate charcoals and pastels, soft lighting, DJ booth and new sound system. 'The Venue', with a capacity of 600 standing or 350 seated, has played host to the finest national & international acts including David Gray, David Kitt, Super Furry Animals and Van Morrison.

Credit Cards: V. MC.
Capacity: 600
Children Friendly: 9.30am-6pm

ROCK, DANCE, TRAD, WORLD, METAL, JAZZ	m	t	w	t	f	s	s
	●	●	●	●	●	●	●

OPENING HOURS:
7 days a week • 9.30am - 2.30am

Viperoom Theatre Bar & Club

5 Aston Quay, Temple Bar, Dublin 2
Tel: 672 5566/7 Fax: 672 5388
E-mail: info@viperoom.ie

The Viperoom Theatre Bar & Club, situated in Temple Bar,
Dublin City-Centre, is a late night venue, set on two levels.

The Viperoom Theatre Bar, decorated with a contemporary
twist, creates the perfect easy-going atmosphere to sit back and
appreciate the staged live music of jazz, salsa, rhythm 'n blues.

The Viperoom Club, decorated in rich reds and purples, with
comfortable seating, is where the DJ ups the pace for dancing;
playing funky, chart and rhythm 'n blues.

Both levels are available for private/exclusive hire, with
catering arranged on request.

Credit Cards: V. MC. AE. L
Capacity: 250

		m	t	w	t	f	s	s
LIVE DJ								
LIVE MUSIC		●	●	●	●	●	●	●

OPENING HOURS:
7 nights 8.00pm-3.30am

pub finder

chic

musical

cabaret

gay

NORTH

NTOWN ROAD

MANOR STREET

STREET

HALLIDAY RD

INFIRMARY ROAD

BRUNSWICK ST

ARBOUR HILL

NORTH KIN

BLACKHALL PL

QUEEN ST

SMITHFIELD

BOW ST

CHURCH STREET

PARKGATE STREET

BENBURB STREET

WOLFE TONE QUAY

ELLIS QY

ARRAN QUAY

CHA

VICTORIA QUAY

USHERS ISL

USHERS QUAY

INN

OAD

STEVENS LANE

WALTING ST

BRIDGEFOOT ST

BRIDGE ST

ME

THOMAS STREET

HIGH ST

ST JAMES'S STREET

RAINSFORD ST

MEATH ST

FRANCIS STREET

MARROWBONE LANE

PIMLICO

THE COOM

ARDEE ST

MANGAN ROAD

CLANBRAS

SUFFERIN AVE

CIRCUIA R

CLANBRASSIL ST

LDS CROSS RD

SOU

SKERRIES

BLANCHARDSTOWN

MALAHIDE

43 17

HOWTH

1

8

CITY CENTRE

TALLAGHT

DUN LAOGHAIRE

40 23

45

26

OAD